Leadership
and the
One Minute
Manager™

Leadership
and the
One Minute
Manager

Kenneth Blanchard, Ph.D.
Co-Author of The One Minute Manager
Patricia Zigarmi, Ed.D.
Drea Zigarmi, Ed.D.

HarperCollinsBusiness

HarperCollins Business
An Imprint of HarperCollins*Publishers*
77–85 Fulham Palace Road,
Hammersmith, London W6 8JB

www.**fire**and**water**.com/business

This paperback edition 1994
11   13   15   12   10

Previously published in paperback by Fontana 1987
Reprinted ten times

First published in Great Britain by
Collins 1986

ISBN 0 00 710341 7

Set in Times

Printed and bound in Great Britain by
Omnia Books Ltd, Glasgow

Contents

Dedicated
to
Paul Hersey
for
his genius and creativity
in our development of
Situational Leadership
and
his many other important contributions
to the field of
Applied Behavioural Sciences

●01 *The Symbol*

The One Minute Manager's
symbol – a one-minute readout
from the face of a modern digital
watch – is intended to remind
each of us to take a minute out
of our day to look into the faces
of the people we manage. And to
realise that *they* are our most
important resources.

01 *Introduction*

In this episode of the One Minute Manager, an entrepreneur bemoans the fact that she lacks devoted
hardworking talent in her organisation. As a result,
she complains that she has to do most of the work
herself. She seeks advice from the One Minute
Manager who suggests she should work 'smarter –
not harder'. In the process the entrepreneur learns
from the One Minute Manager how to use 'Different
Strokes for Different Folks' and become a Situational
Leader.

The acceptance of Situational Leadership as a
practical, easy-to-understand-and-apply approach to
managing and motivating people has been widespread
throughout the world over the last decade and a half.
Paul Hersey and I first described Situational Leadership as the 'life-cycle theory of leadership' and then
wrote about it extensively in our Prentice-Hall text
*Management of Organisational Behaviour: Utilising
Human Resources*, now in its fourth edition. Since then,
Situational Leadership has been taught to managers
at all levels of most of the *Fortune* 500 companies, as
well as to managers in fast-growing entrepreneurial
organisations.

Thus it is only fitting that the fourth book in the One Minute Manager Library be devoted to my thinking about Situational Leadership and be written with Pat and Drea Zigarmi. The Zigarmis have been teaching, rethinking, and implementing Situational Leadership concepts with me for over ten years.

Those of you who know Situational Leadership will see that we've made a number of changes in the model – changes that reflect conversations with our colleagues at Blanchard Training and Development, Inc., our own experience, and the ideas managers have shared with us. This book marks for us a new generation of Situational Leadership thinking, which is why we now call it *Situational Leadership II.*

Pat, Drea, and I hope this will be a book that you will read and reread until using a variety of leadership styles in directing and supporting the work of others becomes second nature to you in your roles as a manager and as a parent.

Kenneth Blanchard, Ph.D.

THE One Minute Manager had a phone call one day from a woman who said she was an 'entrepreneur'. He was glad to hear from her because he knew that the country was in the midst of an entrepreneurial boom and that a large share of the growth in new businesses came from women.

The entrepreneur explained that she was having a hard time finding people who were willing to work as hard as she was.

'I seem to have to do everything. I feel like the Lone Ranger,' said the entrepreneur.

'What you have to do,' said the One Minute Manager, 'is learn to delegate.'

'But my staff are not ready,' said the entrepreneur.

'Then you need to train them,' said the One Minute Manager.

'But I don't have time,' said the entrepreneur.

'If that's the case,' grinned the One Minute Manager, 'you do have a problem. Why don't you come over this afternoon and we'll have a talk.'

THAT afternoon when the entrepreneur arrived at the One Minute Manager's office she found him talking to his secretary at her desk.

'Thank you for agreeing to meet me,' said the entrepreneur as she joined the One Minute Manager in his office.

'It's my pleasure,' said the One Minute Manager. 'I've heard that you have been very successful in a number of ventures. What do you think it takes to be successful?'

'It's really quite easy,' smiled the entrepreneur. 'All you have to do is work half a day. You can work either the first twelve hours or the second twelve hours.'

The One Minute Manager had a good laugh. Then he said, 'While I think the amount of time and effort you put into work is important, I'm afraid too many people think there is a direct relationship between amount of work and success – the more time you put in, the more successful you will be.'

'I thought you would say that,' said the entrepreneur. 'In fact, I understand one of your favourite quotes is:

*

Don't
Work
Harder –
Work
Smarter

*

'Absolutely,' said the One Minute Manager. 'Before talking about some of my thoughts on working smarter, let me ask you one more question.'

'Fire away,' said the entrepreneur.

'You call yourself an entrepreneur,' said the One Minute Manager. 'What does that mean to you?'

The entrepreneur smiled and said, 'A friend of mine described beautifully what it means to be an entrepreneur. He told me he once took his managing director to the top of a hill that overlooked the city. It was a beautiful view.

'He said to his managing director, "Do you see that ridge down there? Wouldn't that be a great place to build a house?"

' "It certainly would."

' "Can you imagine a swimming pool over to the right? Wouldn't that be wonderful?" continued my friend.

' "Really marvellous," said the managing director.

' "How about a tennis court to the left?" said my friend.

' "What a setting," said the managing director.

' "Let me tell you one thing," said my friend. "If you continue to work as hard as you have and accomplish all the goals we have set, I guarantee that some day – some day all of that will be mine." '

'That's beautiful,' said the One Minute Manager with a big smile on his face. 'But I think that story illustrates some of your problems with managing and motivating others.'

'What do you mean?' asked the entrepreneur.

'LET me explain it this way,' said the One Minute Manager. 'I would imagine your organization looks like a pyramid with you, as the Chairman, at the top and all the hourly employees at the bottom. In between are several levels of management.'

'That's the way it's organised,' said the entrepreneur. 'Is there something wrong with a pyramidal organisation?'

'No,' said the One Minute Manager. 'There is nothing wrong with it as an organisational model. The trouble comes when you think in a pyramid.'

'I don't think I follow you,' said the entrepreneur.

'When you think in a pyramid,' continued the One Minute Manager, 'the assumption is that everyone works for the person above them on the organisational ladder. As a result, managers are thought to be "responsible" for planning, organising, and evaluating everything that happens in the organisation while their staff are supposed to be "responsive to the directives of management". That's why people like you end up thinking managers do all the work.'

'How should it be?' asked the entrepreneur.

'I prefer to turn the pyramid upside down so that top managers are at the bottom,' said the One Minute Manager. 'When that happens there is a subtle, but powerful, twist in who is responsible and who should be responsive to whom.'

'In other words, you're saying managers should work for their staff,' said the entrepreneur, 'and not the reverse.'

'Precisely,' said the One Minute Manager. 'If you think your staff are responsible and that your job is to be responsive, you really work hard to provide them with the resources and working conditions they need to accomplish the goals you've agreed to. You realise your job is not to do all the work yourself or to sit back and wait to "catch them doing something wrong", but to roll up your sleeves and help them win. If they win, you win.'

'But as I told you earlier,' said the entrepreneur, 'I don't have time to be responsive to the needs of all my staff.'

'You don't have to work closely with all your staff,' said the One Minute Manager, 'only those who need help.'

'You mean you treat people differently?' wondered the entrepreneur.

'Absolutely,' said the One Minute Manager. 'There's a saying we use around here that says it all:

*

*Different Strokes
For
Different Folks*

*

'**I**F that's true,' wondered the entrepreneur, 'how do you treat your staff differently?'

'Why don't you talk to some of them?' asked the One Minute Manager. 'They can tell you about my various leadership styles.'

'Leadership styles?' echoed the entrepreneur.

'Your leadership style is the way you supervise or work with someone,' said the One Minute Manager. 'It's how you behave when you're trying to influence the performance of others.'

'Is your leadership style the way you think you behave,' asked the entrepreneur, 'or the way others say you behave?'

'Let me explain it this way,' said the One Minute Manager. 'If you think you are an empathetic, staff-oriented manager, but your staff think you are a hard-nosed, task-oriented person, whose perception of reality will they use – yours or their own?'

'Obviously their own,' said the entrepreneur.

'Right,' said the One Minute Manager. 'Your perception of how you behave is interesting but it tells you only how you *intend* to act. Unless it matches the perceptions of others it is not very helpful. That's why I want you to talk to some of my staff. They'll tell you the truth about my leadership style so you can see if I really treat people differently.'

'Sounds good to me,' said the entrepreneur. 'But I suppose you won't help me decide which ones I should talk to.'

'No,' chuckled the One Minute Manager. 'As you know, I seldom make decisions for people.' With that said, he leaned over and spoke into the office intercom. His secretary, Mrs Johnson, came in moments later and handed the entrepreneur a list of six names.

'Here a list of the people who report to me,' said the One Minute Manager. 'Pick any name. Talk to any of them.'

'Let me start with Larry McKenzie,' said the entrepreneur as she looked at the list. 'Then he can take me around to the others I want to see.'

'I'm sure he will,' said the One Minute Manager, smiling.

'I'll get directions to his office from Mrs Johnson,' said the entrepreneur. 'See you later.'

'I'll look forward to it,' said the One Minute Manager.

THE entrepreneur was in a good mood as she headed toward Larry McKenzie's office. She was glad she had decided to come to see the One Minute Manager. 'I have a feeling I will learn some useful things here,' she thought to herself.

When she got to McKenzie's office, she found a relaxed-looking man in his early thirties. He was the director in charge of training for the company.

After they exchanged greetings, McKenzie got right to the point. 'I understand you've been visiting the boss. What can I do for you?'

'I'm interested in finding out how the One Minute Manager works with you,' said the entrepreneur. 'Would you call him a participative manager? I've been reading a lot about participative management.'

'He's far from participative with me,' said McKenzie. 'In fact, he is very directive with me. Training is his baby. So my job is essentially to implement his ideas.'

'Does he assign you tasks and then just leave you alone?' wondered the entrepreneur.

'No,' said McKenzie. 'He assigns me tasks and then works very closely with me. At the moment I am an extension of the One Minute Manager in this area.'

'Don't you resent that?' asked the entrepreneur. 'It sounds pretty autocratic to me.'

'Not at all,' said McKenzie. 'I was in personnel – in wage and salary administration to be exact – before I got this position three months ago. I jumped at the opportunity to move into training because working with the One Minute Manager would give me a chance to learn the training area from the bottom. He is considered a real pro when it comes to managing and training people. So when he works with me, he helps me plan what he wants me to do. He's very clear about how he wants me to do it, and I always know where I stand and what he thinks about my performance because of the frequent meetings we have.'

'Do you think he will ever let you make any decisions on your own?' asked the entrepreneur.

'Yes,' said McKenzie, 'as I learn the ropes. But you know, it's hard to make good decisions when I don't know a lot about the job yet. Just now I'm glad that the One Minute Manager wants to be involved. I'm excited about my job and as I gain experience, I'm sure I'll take more responsibility.'

'Does the One Minute Manager treat everyone who reports to him the way he manages you?' asked the entrepreneur.

'No,' said McKenzie. 'Let me take you next door and introduce you to Cathy Murrow, our director of finance. The One Minute Manager treats her very differently.'

With that McKenzie got up and started towards the door. The entrepreneur followed closely behind.

When they got to Cathy Murrow's office, the entrepreneur met a thoughtful-looking woman in her middle forties. After thanking Larry McKenzie, the entrepreneur sat down with Murrow.

'Mr McKenzie said that the One Minute Manager supervises you differently than he does him,' began the entrepreneur. 'Is that true?'

'Absolutely,' said Murrow. 'We operate as colleagues in the financial area. The One Minute Manager never tells me what to do but together we arrive at the direction we want to take.'

'Sounds like he is very participative with you,' said the entrepreneur.

'Very much so,' said Murrow. 'I get a lot of support, encouragement, and praise from the One Minute Manager. What I find him doing is listening to me and drawing me out. He also shares lots of information about the whole company with me so I can make better decisions about what to do in finance. It's a perfect working relationship for me. I've been working in finance for over fifteen years so it is good to be treated as a competent, contributing member of a team. I've worked for some other people who certainly didn't make me feel like that.'

'From talking to you,' said the entrepreneur, 'I'm beginning to believe that the One Minute Manager is either autocratic or democratic. With Larry McKenzie he is very directive and authoritarian, and with you he's very supportive and participative.'

'Don't draw any conclusions about these being his only two styles,' said Murrow, 'until you talk to John DaLapa, our director of operations.'

'You mean the One Minute Manager treats Mr DaLapa differently than he does either you or Mr McKenzie?' asked the entrepreneur.

'He certainly does,' said Cathy Murrow. 'John is down the hall. Why don't I take you down to chat with him?'

'That would be helpful,' said the entrepreneur.

When Murrow and the entrepreneur reached John DaLapa's office, he was talking to the One Minute Manager.

'I'd better get out of here,' laughed the One Minute Manager, 'or you will think I am prejudicing your sample.'

'He doesn't scare me,' smiled DaLapa as he shook hands with the entrepreneur. He nodded at Murrow and the One Minute Manager. 'I'll tell her the real truth.'

The entrepreneur was impressed by the light-hearted, supportive atmosphere she found in the company. Everyone seemed to enjoy each other's company and respect one another.

When Murrow and the One Minute Manager left, John DaLapa invited the entrepreneur to sit down. 'Well, what can I do for you?' he asked.

'Cathy Murrow says that the One Minute Manager supervises you differently from the way he manages either McKenzie or her. Is that true?'

'Well, I don't know about that,' said DaLapa. 'It's not easy for me to describe his style.'

'What do you mean?' asked the entrepreneur.

'Well, my job is fairly complicated,' DaLapa said. 'I'm ultimately responsible for all of production. That means I supervise and control each part of the operation. I'm also responsible for inspection and quality control, as well as for hiring and firing. What I find is that the One Minute Manager uses one style with me on certain parts of my job and another style with me on other parts. For example, on the operations end of my job he literally leaves me alone, but it took him a while before he would do that. The One Minute Manager built this company from the ground up. Because he knows the technical side of the business as well as I do, he's come to respect and trust my judgment on technical matters. Now he just says, "Keep me informed but that's your area – you run with the ball. You're the technical expert around here." '

'You mean he doesn't discuss things with you or tell you what to do or tell you how to solve a particular problem?' questioned the entrepreneur.

'No,' said DaLapa. 'Not as far as the technical part of my job goes. But his style is completely different when it comes to the people part of my job. He insists that I consult him before I implement any new personnel programmes or policies. He wants to know exactly what I intend to do.'

'Does he tell you what to do in those areas?' asked the entrepreneur.

'He always tells me his opinion,' said DaLapa, 'if that's what you mean. But he usually asks mine, too.'

'If there is a difference in your opinions and you can't come to agreement, who decides?' wondered the entrepreneur.

'The One Minute Manager decides.'

'Is it disconcerting when he treats you one way sometimes and another way at other times?' asked the entrepreneur.

'Not at all,' said DaLapa. 'I love the freedom he gives me on the operations part of my job. After all, I started as a technician here and worked my way up the ladder to my present position. Over the twenty years I've been here, I have always kept on top of our technology.'

'Wouldn't you like to be treated in the same way in the personnel area?' asked the entrepreneur.

'Not really,' said DaLapa. 'With people I'm sometimes like a bull in a china shop. In fact, some people claim I knock down the door and then ask if I can come in. So I'm not always confident about my ability to deal with people. That's why I welcome the One Minute Manager's suggestions.'

'It sounds like the One Minute Manager is an eclectic manager,' said the entrepreneur, 'one who is able to choose from a variety of styles.'

'I wouldn't say that to him,' said DaLapa.

'Why?' wondered the entrepreneur.

'Because he defines an eclectic as someone who has both feet planted in mid-air,' laughed DaLapa.

'Well, what kind of leader would you call him?' asked the entrepreneur.

'A situational leader,' said DaLapa. 'He changes his style depending on the person he is working with and on the situation.'

'**A** situational leader . . .' That phrase kept going through the entrepreneur's mind as she headed back to the One Minute Manager's office. When she arrived, Mrs Johnson ushered her in to see the One Minute Manager.

'Well, how did I do?' asked the One Minute Manager.

'Fine,' said the entrepreneur. 'Your philosophy of Different Strokes for Different Folks is alive and well. And what's more, your folks don't seem to mind being treated differently. How can I become a situational leader?'

'You need to learn three skills,' said the One Minute Manager.

'I knew you would have it down to some simple formula,' the entrepreneur teased.

'I'm not sure it's so simple,' chuckled the One Minute Manager, 'but there are three skills involved. You have to learn to use a variety of leadership styles flexibly. You have to learn how to diagnose the needs of the people you supervise. And you have to learn how to come to some agreements with them, to contract with them for the leadership style they need from you. In other words, the three skills are: *flexibility*, *diagnosis*, and *contracting*.'

'Sounds fascinating,' said the entrepreneur. 'Where do I start?'

'We usually start by teaching people about flexibility,' said the One Minute Manager. 'That's why I sent you to talk to some of my staff – to find out about the different leadership styles I use with them.'

'I thought I had your styles worked out until I talked to John DaLapa,' said the entrepreneur.

'What do you mean?' asked the One Minute Manager.

'I thought you were either autocratic or democratic,' said the entrepreneur, 'but that didn't fit with DaLapa.'

'That always surprises people,' said the One Minute Manager. 'For a long time people thought there were only two leadership styles – autocratic and democratic. In fact, people used to shout at each other from these two extremes, insisting that one style was better than the other. Democratic managers were accused of being too soft and easy, while their autocratic counterparts were often called too tough and domineering. But I have always felt that managers who restricted themselves to either extreme were only "half a manager".'

'What makes someone a whole manager?' asked the entrepreneur.

'A whole manager is flexible and is able to use four different leadership styles,' said the One Minute Manager as he showed the entrepreneur a sheet of paper.

THE
FOUR BASIC
LEADERSHIP STYLES
ARE:

Style 1: **DIRECTING**

THE LEADER PROVIDES SPECIFIC INSTRUCTIONS AND
CLOSELY SUPERVISES TASK ACCOMPLISHMENT.

Style 2: **COACHING**

THE LEADER CONTINUES TO DIRECT AND CLOSELY
SUPERVISE TASK ACCOMPLISHMENT, BUT ALSO EXPLAINS
DECISIONS, SOLICITS SUGGESTIONS, AND SUPPORTS
PROGRESS.

Style 3: **SUPPORTING**

THE LEADER FACILITATES AND SUPPORTS SUBORDINATES'
EFFORTS TOWARD TASK ACCOMPLISHMENT AND SHARES
RESPONSIBILITY FOR DECISION-MAKING WITH THEM.

Style 4: **DELEGATING**

THE LEADER TURNS OVER RESPONSIBILITY FOR DECISION-
MAKING AND PROBLEM-SOLVING TO SUBORDINATES.

As the entrepreneur studied the information on the sheet of paper, the One Minute Manager began to explain it.

'These four styles consist of different combinations of two basic leadership behaviours that a manager can use when trying to influence someone else: *Directive Behaviour* and *Supportive Behaviour*. Three words can be used to define Directive Behaviour: STRUCTURE, CONTROL, and SUPERVISE. Different words are used to describe Supportive Behaviour: PRAISE, LISTEN, and FACILITATE.'

'Directive behaviour seems to be related to autocratic leadership,' said the entrepreneur.

'Precisely,' said the One Minute Manager. 'It's really one-way communication. You tell the person what, when, where, and how to do something and then you closely supervise the person on the problem or task.'

'That sounds exactly like the way you are managing Larry McKenzie,' said the entrepreneur. 'You're using a Style 1.'

'You're right,' said the One Minute Manager. 'We refer to Style 1 as *directing* because when you use that style you are high on directive behaviour but low on supportive behaviour. You tell the person what the goal is and what a good job looks like, but you also lay out a step-by-step plan about how the task is to be accomplished. You solve the problem. You make the decisions; the subordinate carries out your ideas.'

'But that's not the style you've been using with Cathy Murrow. You've been more supportive, more democratic.'

'Absolutely,' said the One Minute Manager. 'That's why we call Style 3, which is high on supportive behaviour but low on directive behaviour, *supporting*. You support subordinates' efforts, listen to their suggestions and facilitate their interactions with others. And to build up their confidence and motivation, you encourage and praise. Rarely do Style 3 managers talk about how they would go about solving a particular problem or accomplishing a particular task. They help their subordinates reach their own solutions by asking questions that expand their thinking and encourage risk-taking.'

'But isn't it inconsistent to treat Mr McKenzie one way and Ms Murrow another, not to mention Mr DaLapa?' asked the young woman.

'I believe in being consistent, but I think I have a different definition of consistency. It sounds as if your definition is "treating everybody the same way". My definition is "using the same leadership style in similar situations".'

'But isn't it unfair to treat people differently?' asked the entrepreneur.

The One Minute Manager pointed to a plaque on the wall.

*

There Is Nothing
So Unequal
As The Equal Treatment
Of
Unequals

*

'You must be a fan of Emerson,' said the young woman. 'He said, "A foolish consistency is the hobgoblin of little minds." '

The One Minute Manager smiled. 'That's always been one of my favourite sayings.'

'Just to clarify in my mind the four styles you described, could you give me an example of each?' asked the entrepreneur.

'Certainly,' said the One Minute Manager. 'Suppose there was some noise in the outside office that was bothering us. If I said to you, "Please go out now and tell Mrs Johnson to get those people to move their conversation down the hall and when you've done that report back to me," what leadership style would that be?'

'A *directing* style,' said the entrepreneur. 'How would you deal with the noise if you wanted to use a *supporting* style?'

'I'd say something like "There's noise in the outside office that's bothering us – what do you think we could do about it?" '

'I see,' said the entrepreneur. 'What about Style 2?'

'*Coaching* combines both direction and support,' said the One Minute Manager. 'If I wanted to use a coaching style in handling the noise I would say, "There's a lot of noise in the outside office that's bothering us. I think you should go outside and tell Mrs Johnson to ask those people to move their conversation down the hall. Do you have any questions or suggestions?" '

'So with a *coaching* style,' said the entrepreneur, 'you begin to engage in two-way communication by asking for suggestions. Does the manager end up making the final decision?'

'Absolutely,' said the One Minute Manager, 'but you get input from others. You also provide a lot of support because some of the ideas they suggest are good and as a manager you always want to reinforce initiative and risk-taking. That's where the listening and encouraging come in. You're trying to teach your staff how to evaluate their own work.'

'So Style 2 means you consult the subordinate. What if you were using Style 4 – *delegating*?' asked the entrepreneur. 'I would imagine you would just say, "That noise outside is bothering us. Would you please take care of it?" '

'That would be perfect for a *delegating* style,' said the One Minute Manager. 'In Style 4 you are turning over responsibility for day-to-day decision-making and problem-solving to the person doing the task. So you can see that with the same problem and the same task – to do something about the noise – you can use any of the four leadership styles.'

'Of the four leadership styles,' asked the entrepreneur, 'isn't there a "best" leadership style? I hear a lot about how important it is to use a participative management style.'

'**M**ANY people believe that,' said the One Minute Manager. 'But that's where the word "situational" comes into play. A participative-supporting style may be a better approach in some situations, but not in others.'

'I can't imagine when an autocratic-directing style would be appropriate,' said the entrepreneur.

'There are several situations,' said the One Minute Manager. 'Suppose you were at a meeting and the room burst into flames. Would you ask everyone to break into small groups to discuss what was the best way out of the room and then have each group report back so that the whole group could agree on the best course of action?'

'Absolutely not,' laughed the entrepreneur. 'I'd say, "There's the door; everyone follow me." '

'So a *directing* style is appropriate when a decision has to be made quickly and the stakes are high,' said the One Minute Manager.

'I'll buy that example,' said the entrepreneur. 'In what other situations would a *directing* style be appropriate?'

'Suppose you take on someone who has little experience but, you think, real potential for learning a certain job,' said the One Minute Manager. 'Does it make sense to ask that person what, when, where, and how to do things?'

'Not unless you're interested in pooling ignorance,' said the entrepreneur. 'I understand what you're getting at now. *Directing* is also appropriate for inexperienced people who you think have the potential to be self-directive.'

'Most definitely,' said the One Minute Manager. '*Directing* might also be appropriate for someone who has some skills but doesn't know the company – its priorities, policies, or ways of doing business.'

'Don't people often resent direction and close supervision?' wondered the entrepreneur.

'Not usually in the beginning,' said the One Minute Manager. 'When they are first learning a task, most people are *enthusiastic beginners*. They're ready for any help you can give them. After all, they want to perform well.'

'Do you really think people want to perform well?' the entrepreneur asked. 'I've observed a lot of people in organisations who appear to be trading time on the job to satisfy needs elsewhere. They seem to be working just for the money. They don't care whether the organisation accomplishes its goals or not.'

'You are right,' said the One Minute Manager. 'There are people – too many I'm sad to say – who don't seem to care and are just putting in time for a cheque at the end of the month. But if you could go back and observe them when they were first starting a new job, I doubt if you would see that lack of commitment. I think people lose their commitment only after they realise that good performance doesn't make a difference.'

'What do you mean?' asked the entrepreneur.

'I mean,' said the One Minute Manager, 'that good performance often goes unrecognised. When people do something good, their managers don't say anything. When they make a mistake, they hear about it right away.'

'The old "leave alone-hit" leadership style I've heard people say you talk about all the time,' smiled the entrepreneur.

'I now call it "seagull management",' said the One Minute Manager. 'Seagull managers fly in, make a lot of noise, dump on everyone, and then fly out.'

The entrepreneur and the One Minute Manager had a good laugh because they both knew how true that was.

'So I think it's how inexperienced people are managed that causes them to lose their commitment,' said the One Minute Manager. 'Once you've lost commitment, providing direction is not enough; you also have to provide support and encouragement.'

'Now you're talking about a *coaching* style, aren't you?' suggested the entrepreneur.

'Yes,' said the One Minute Manager. 'A *coaching* style works best when disillusionment sets in.'

'Disillusionment?' echoed the entrepreneur.

'Haven't you noticed,' said the One Minute Manager, 'that as people begin to work on a task, they often find it harder to master than they thought it was going to be, so they lose interest. Or maybe the drop in commitment comes because they don't think the rewards are going to be worth all the effort. Or maybe they aren't getting the direction they need – in fact, they're continually getting criticised. Or progress is so slow or nonexistent that they lose confidence in their ability to learn to do the task well. When this disillusionment happens, when the initial excitement wears off, the best style is a *coaching* style, which is high on direction and support.'

'You want to continue to direct because they still need to build skills?' the entrepreneur asked.

'Yes,' said the One Minute Manager. 'But you also want to listen to their concerns, provide perspective, and praise progress. And you want to involve them in decision-making as much as you can because that's how you'll build back their commitment.'

'You make it sound as if everyone gets disillusioned at some point when they're learning a new task or taking over a new project,' the entrepreneur added.

'Some people more than others,' said the One Minute Manager. 'It depends on how much praise the manager provides and how available the manager is. But I'm getting ahead of myself.'

'Interesting,' said the entrepreneur. 'So a *directing* leadership style is better with *enthusiastic beginners* whereas *coaching* is the right style for *disillusioned learners*.'

'Right,' said the One Minute Manager. 'What kind of people do you think dislike *directing* or *coaching*?'

'Experienced people,' said the entrepreneur. 'They would probably like a more participative management style.'

'You've got it,' said the One Minute Manager. 'Experienced people like to be listened to and supported. I think you talked to Cathy Murrow. She responds well to a *supporting* style because even though she's experienced and competent she's sometimes a *reluctant contributor*. When I ask her to take on a project, she has a lot of ideas, but she'll often want to test her ideas out with me first. She wants to be involved in decision-making, but she sometimes doesn't have as much faith in her ideas as I do. She needs recognition, which a *supporting* style provides. And yet a *supporting* style is not a universally good style.'

'For example?' asked the entrepreneur.

'We had a classic example with a close friend of ours,' said the One Minute Manager. 'His marriage was in trouble – he and his wife were putting each other down all the time. Finally we persuaded them to go to a marriage guidance counsellor and then we sat back believing we'd done what we could.'

'Hadn't you?' asked the entrepreneur.

'No,' continued the One Minute Manager. 'We didn't ask them what kind of counsellor they were going to. They went to a supportive, nondirective counsellor.'

'Well, what happened?' the entrepreneur wanted to know.

'They paid the counsellor twenty pounds an hour,' said the One Minute Manager, 'while they screamed and yelled at each other. During those discussions the counsellor would do nothing but rub his beard and say, "Hmmm, I sense some anger here." They had three sessions with him and split up.'

'What you're suggesting is that they needed a good directive counsellor,' said the entrepreneur, 'one who would tell them exactly what they needed to do to start to turn their marriage around. But I'll bet the counsellor they went to was effective with other couples.'

'Right,' said the One Minute Manager. 'Their counsellor was very effective with couples who had problems they could solve themselves, with couples who needed someone who could listen and support them while they problem-solved. It sounds as if you're convinced now that there is no one best leadership style.'

'You're getting to me,' the entrepreneur said, smiling. 'But what about *delegating*? How does it fit in?'

'*Delegating* is appropriate for people who are *peak performers* – people who are competent and committed. Therefore they don't need much direction, and they are also able to provide their own support,' said the One Minute Manager.

'You mean they praise themselves?' asked the entrepreneur.

'In many cases they do,' said the One Minute Manager. 'When you go to see them, they often take you on "praising tours" – pointing out all the things they and their staff have done right. Top performers don't need much supervision or praise as long as they know how well they are doing. I heard a good story the other day that emphasises the importance of delegating.'

'What story is that?' asked the entrepreneur.

'I thought you would never ask,' laughed the One Minute Manager.

'One day a little girl asked her mother, "Mummy, why does Daddy bring so much work home at night?"

' "Because he doesn't have time to finish it at work," answered the mother.

' "Then why don't they put him in a slower group?" asked the little girl.'

'THAT'S a great story,' laughed the entrepreneur. 'If the little girl had known about Situational Leadership, she could have asked why Daddy didn't delegate more.

'I think I'm convinced now that there's no best way to influence others,' said the entrepreneur, 'yet I need some more information to help me decide when to use which leadership style in what situation. You gave me some good thoughts but I'm afraid your examples depend upon my ability to determine whether my staff have all the skills and experience they need to do the job they're assigned and my sense of whether they want to or believe they can do it.'

'That skill of diagnosing a situation before you act is the key to being a situational leader,' agreed the One Minute Manager. 'And yet most managers aren't willing to stop for a minute to try to decide what needs to be done before they act. They just keep running.' As he pointed to a plaque on the wall, the One Minute Manager said, 'That's why I keep that reminder.' It read:

*

When I
Slow Down

I Go
Faster

*

'So I should think before I act,' said the entrepreneur.

'That's what diagnosing is all about,' said the One Minute Manager. 'Why don't you go and talk to Alice Marshall, one of my other key people, about developing your diagnostic skills.'

'That would be great,' said the entrepreneur. 'But let me review my notes with you just to make sure I understand all about flexibility.'

'Good idea,' said the One Minute Manager as the entrepreneur showed him her notes.

LEADERSHIP STYLE is how you behave when you are trying to influence the performance of someone else. Leadership Style is a combination of directive and supportive behaviours.

DIRECTIVE BEHAVIOUR

Involves: clearly telling people what to do, how to do it, where to do it, and when to do it, and then closely supervising their performance.

SUPPORTIVE BEHAVIOUR

Involves: listening to people, providing support and encouragement for their efforts, and then facilitating their involvement in problem-solving and decision-making.

There are four leadership styles: *Directing*, *Coaching*, *Supporting*, and *Delegating* BUT . . . THERE IS NO ONE BEST LEADERSHIP STYLE.

As the One Minute Manager read the entrepreneur's notes he smiled. 'You're ready for Alice, but before I ring her, let me give you this summary of the four basic leadership styles.'

While the entrepreneur studied the chart, the One Minute Manager rang Alice Marshall.

High Supportive and Low Directive Behaviour **S3** **SUPPORTING**	High Directive and High Supportive Behaviour **S2** **COACHING**
Low Supportive and Low Directive Behaviour **S4** **DELEGATING**	High Directive and Low Supportive Behaviour **S1** **DIRECTING**

(HIGH) ↑ SUPPORTIVE BEHAVIOUR

(LOW) ← DIRECTIVE BEHAVIOUR → (HIGH)

ALICE Marshall was waiting outside her office to greet the entrepreneur when she arrived. 'So you want to work on your diagnostic skills,' she smiled.

'I certainly do,' said the entrepreneur. 'I sense that flexibility is important, but without knowing when to use which leadership style with which people you could get yourself into trouble.'

'Yes you could,' said Marshall. 'I once worked for a manager who was very flexible – he could use all four leadership styles – he just used the wrong style with the wrong people at the wrong time.'

'Really?' asked the entrepreneur.

'Yes,' said Marshall. 'He was always telling his best people what to do because he knew his career depended on them, but they resented it because they already knew what to do. With his poorer performers, he didn't respect them so he left them alone. Since they didn't know what to do, they floundered.'

'I get the impression from your example,' said the entrepreneur, 'that one of the factors you have to diagnose before using a particular leadership style is the person's past performance.'

'Absolutely,' said Marshall, 'and in examining performance you need to look at two ingredients that determine a person's performance or achievement: *competence* and *commitment*. In other words, any time a person is not performing well without your supervision, it is usually a competence problem, a commitment problem, or both.'

'How do you tell whether a person has the competence to do a job?' the entrepreneur wondered.

'*Competence* is a function of *knowledge* and *skills*, which can be gained from *education*, *training*, and/or *experience*,' said Marshall.

'Isn't competence just another word for ability?' asked the entrepreneur.

'Not really,' said Marshall. 'People often use the word ability to mean potential. They talk about "natural" ability to describe why some people seem to be able to acquire certain skills so easily. Competence, on the other hand, can be developed with appropriate direction and support. It's not something you are born with. It's something that is learned.'

'Then how do you determine a person's commitment?' asked the entrepreneur.

'*Commitment* is a combination of *confidence* and *motivation*. Confidence is a measure of a person's self-assuredness – a feeling of being able to do a task well without much supervision, whereas motivation is a person's interest in and enthusiasm for doing a task well.'

'Are there times when a person has the competence and confidence to do a job, but no interest?' asked the entrepreneur.

'Yes,' said Marshall. 'Sometimes people lose motivation when they realise it is going to be harder than they thought. Or maybe they feel their efforts aren't being recognised. At other times, people just get bored – they just decide it isn't worth it.'

'I would imagine people can have various combinations of competence and commitment, can't they?' asked the entrepreneur.

'Good point,' said Marshall. 'In fact, four combinations of competence and commitment make up what we call "development level".' Marshall sketched out a diagram on a piece of paper.

THE FOUR DEVELOPMENT LEVELS ARE

HIGH COMPETENCE • HIGH COMMITMENT	HIGH COMPETENCE • VARIABLE COMMITMENT	SOME COMPETENCE • LOW COMMITMENT	LOW COMPETENCE • HIGH COMMITMENT
D4	D3	D2	D1

DEVELOPED ◄─────────────────── DEVELOPING

As the entrepreneur looked at the sketch, she noticed that Marshall had broken down the diagram, which she labelled development level, into four segments: D1, D2, D3, and D4.

'After all my discussions here I can see that people who are at different levels of development would need to be treated differently,' said the entrepreneur.

'That's right,' said Marshall. 'And that is why we have the saying you undoubtedly saw in the One Minute Manager's office: Different Strokes for Different Folks.'

'I would imagine that the people who can work independently, without supervision, are at development levels D3 or D4,' said the entrepreneur.

'Definitely!' said Marshall. 'When they're at those development levels, they have demonstrated the necessary skills and knowledge to perform at a high level. The difference between a D4 and a D3 is commitment. If it's a confidence problem, a D3 needs support, encouragement, and praise. If it's a motivation problem, the leader needs to listen and problem-solve. A D4, however, is confident and self-motivated. People at this development level need fewer praisings from others. They catch themselves doing things right and thus need little, if any, supervision.'

'Probably all they need to know is what the goals are,' said the entrepreneur. 'I like those kinds of people. Why would you even want to hire people at the other development levels?'

'Because good performers are hard to find,' said Marshall. 'They don't just grow on trees. In fact, in more cases than not, you have to train people to be good performers and that involves good diagnostic skills. One of our favourite sayings around here is:

*

*Everyone Has
Peak Performance
Potential –
You Just
Need To Know
Where They Are Coming From
And
Meet Them
There*

*

'So what you mean', said the entrepreneur, 'is that all of us have potential that can be developed.'

'Right,' said Marshall. 'There's nothing negative about being at a lower level of development. All of us have been at a low level of development some time in our lives on some job we have been assigned. Since we'd never done the job before, we lacked the skills to begin to perform immediately at a high level. Our competence and commitment had to be developed.'

'From your sketch it seems that the difference between the other two development levels, D1 and D2, is also commitment,' said the entrepreneur.

'That's true,' said Marshall. 'They both lack competence and thus the necessary skills and experience to perform at a high level without supervision, but the D1 is motivated while the D2 is not. The D1's high commitment comes from an initial sense of excitement about learning something new. A D1 can also be extremely confident, although it may be a false sense of confidence. As people's skills grow, their confidence and motivation often drop. They begin to realise how much more they've got to learn to be able to do a really good job. It's like the old saying: THE MORE I KNOW, THE MORE I REALISE I DON'T KNOW. With coaching, a D2's confidence begins to go back up, as he or she gets positive feedback on results.'

'**I** would imagine a D1 is more dangerous without supervision than a D2 is,' said the entrepreneur.

'Why do you say that?' asked Alice Marshall.

'Because if you delegate to someone who is enthusiastic and confident, but lacks ability and experience,' said the entrepreneur, 'he or she will fail with vigour. Such a person will rush in where angels fear to tread.'

'Good point,' said Marshall. 'If you delegate to a D2, that person will probably not act without further direction because he or she lacks the self-confidence or motivation to take a risk. But a confident person without the necessary competence may not be as cautious.'

'I'm already getting a feel for what leadership style would be appropriate for each development level, each combination of competence and commitment,' said the entrepreneur.

'To help the process along,' said Marshall, pointing to a diagram on her desk, 'look at how we portray the relationship between the four development levels and the four leadership styles the One Minute Manager told you about when he was discussing flexibility.'

DEVELOPMENT LEVEL	APPROPRIATE LEADERSHIP STYLE
D1 Low Competence • High Commitment	**S1** DIRECTING Structure, control, and supervise
D2 Some Competence • Low Commitment	**S2** COACHING Direct and support
D3 High Competence • Variable Commitment	**S3** SUPPORTING Praise, listen, and facilitate
D4 High Competence • High Commitment	**S4** DELEGATING Turn over responsibility for day-to-day decision-making

**LEADERSHIP STYLES
APPROPRIATE FOR
THE VARIOUS
DEVELOPMENT LEVELS**

The entrepreneur examined the relationship between the four development levels and the four leadership styles. Then she looked up.

'That's a very helpful way to remember the relationships – the D's and the S's match up. Let me see if I can summarise:

'*Directing (Style 1) is for people who lack competence but are enthusiastic and committed (D1).* They need direction and supervision to get them started.

'*Coaching (Style 2) is for people who have some competence but lack commitment (D2).* They need direction and supervision because they're still relatively inexperienced. They also need support and praise to build their self-esteem, and involvement in decision-making to restore their commitment.

'*Supporting (Style 3) is for people who have competence but lack confidence or motivation (D3).* They do not need much direction because of their skills, but support is necessary to bolster their confidence and motivation.

'*Delegating (Style 4) is for people who have both competence and commitment (D4).* They are able and willing to work on a project by themselves with little supervision or support.'

When Alice Marshall had finished listening to the entrepreneur's summary, she smiled. 'You learn quickly. That's what diagnosis is all about. I'm glad I shared with you what I know about diagnosis.'

'Thanks for the praise,' said the entrepreneur. 'Once I determine which leadership style to use with someone, do I always use the same style with that person?'

'Why don't you go back and talk with the One Minute Manager about that,' said Marshall. 'Now you're starting to think about changing your leadership style as a person's competence and commitment grows, which is exactly what managers around here try to do. And besides, in the discussion he will show you how the three secrets of One Minute Management – One Minute Goal Setting, One Minute Praisings, and One Minute Reprimands – make the whole concept of Situational Leadership come alive. The One Minute Manager enjoys doing that.'

'I'd love to hear his thoughts,' said the entrepreneur. 'Because it's five o'clock I'll probably have to catch him in the morning. Thanks for your help.'

'It was my pleasure,' said Marshall.

WHEN the entrepreneur got to the One Minute Manager's office the next morning, she found him waiting for her. The minute she saw him, the entrepreneur began to share her excitement about what she had learned.

'It's great to see your enthusiasm,' said the One Minute Manager. 'What questions do you have?'

'Alice Marshall tells me you enjoy showing people the real connections between One Minute Management and Situational Leadership,' said the entrepreneur.

'How do you think they go together?' asked the One Minute Manager.

'Thanks for the *supporting* style,' smiled the entrepreneur, 'but I think I need more direction from you. My impression, though, is that both concepts become more dynamic when used together.'

'I'll agree with that,' said the One Minute Manager. 'Let's look first at how One Minute Goal Setting comes into play, since clear goals are important to people at any development level. You might have got the impression from Alice Marshall that people are at one level of development – whether it be D1, D2, D3, or D4 – for all parts of their job. And yet, that's not true. In fact, some people are more developed in some areas of their job than in others. They can function independently, without supervision, on some tasks but need lots of direction and support on other tasks. Thus you must always assess development level with a specific goal or task in mind. You cannot determine a person's competence or commitment in general, only his or her development level to accomplish a certain goal.'

'You mean people tend to be at different levels of development depending on the specific tasks or goals they are assigned?' wondered the entrepreneur, thinking back to her conversation with John DaLapa.

'**P**RECISELY,' said the One Minute Manager. 'Once you and one of your staff have agreed on three to five goals, then as that person's manager you might have to use different leadership styles in supervising his or her performance on those various goals. For example, let's say that an engineer is competent and confident about handling the technical aspects of his job, but has not demonstrated that same degree of development when it comes to working with his or her budget. As a result, it may be quite appropriate for you as the engineer's manager to provide little direction or support (S4-delegating) on a technical problem, but a great deal of direction and close supervision over the engineer's budget (S1-directing or S2-coaching).'

'That's interesting,' said the entrepreneur. 'That's what you've been doing with John DaLapa, isn't it?'

'You're right,' said the One Minute Manager.

'So as a situational leader, not only should you use different strokes for different folks, but in many cases you need to use *different strokes for the same folks*, depending upon the task,' said the entrepreneur.

'That's very true,' said the One Minute Manager. 'Let me give you a vivid example with my son, Tom. A number of years ago, when he was ten years old, my wife and I got word that he was two to three years ahead of his class in reading, but two to three years behind in maths. When I found out what was happening, I went to see one of his teachers.'

'One of his teachers?' echoed the entrepreneur.

'Tom was in an "open school",' said the One Minute Manager. 'There were one hundred and ten kids in the class, and four or five teachers worked with them in a large open space. When I went to see the teachers, I said to them, "How do you treat Tom differently in reading versus maths?"'

'They said, "What do you mean?"'

'I said, "What do you do during reading?"'

'They said, "Do you see those files on the far wall? Every child has his or her own reading file. When it's reading time, the children go over, get their files out, take them back to their desks, and begin to read where they left off. If they have any questions, they raise their hands and one of us comes over to help them."'

'What leadership style do you think they were using with Tom in reading?' asked the One Minute Manager.

'*Delegating*,' said the entrepreneur. 'He got his own folder and he decided when he needed help.'

'What development level do you think he was at in reading?' questioned the One Minute Manager.

'D4, I would imagine,' said the entrepreneur.

'Absolutely,' said the One Minute Manager. 'He loved reading and was very good at it. As a result, a *delegating* style was right.'

'Then I said to the teachers, "What do you do in maths?"'

'The teachers said, 'See those files on the other wall. Every child has his own maths file. When it's time for maths the children go over, get their files out, take them back to their desks, and begin to do their maths where they left off. If they have any questions, they raise their hands and a teacher comes to help them."

' "How is that working with Tom in maths?" I asked.

' "Horribly," they said. "We're really worried about him."

'I said, "You should be! I'm disappointed in the approach you've been taking with him in maths. Didn't anyone in training college ever tell you that you might have to use a different teaching style with the same child in different subjects?"'

'What leadership style do you think they were using with Tom in maths?'

'*Delegating*,' said the entrepreneur.

'What development level do you think he was at in maths?' asked the One Minute Manager.

'A much lower development level, I assume,' said the entrepreneur.

'That's right,' said the One Minute Manager. 'He was a D2. He didn't like maths because he wasn't very good at it. As a result, the *delegating* style wasn't working. In fact, it was more "abdicating" than *delegating*.'

'Then I asked, "Which one of you has the reputation of being the most traditional teacher?" An older teacher, Mrs McBride, smiled. She had been a teacher for thirty years before her school moved over to (and this was her quote) "This crazy open school system." I remember going past Mrs McBride's classroom one time at twelve-fifteen when she was in a small elementary school that didn't have a dining hall. The door was open and thirty ten-year-olds were sitting silently at their desks eating their lunches while Mrs McBride played Beethoven on the record player.'

'I bet that was a new definition of control for you,' said the entrepreneur.

'It certainly was,' smiled the One Minute Manager. 'Mrs McBride was a beautiful example of a directive leadership style. Across the hall was another classroom. The door was shut but there was a little window in the door. I looked through the window and it looked like a zoo in there. The kids were running all over the place, up on the desks and chairs. Mrs Jones, the teacher, who is a wonderful person, was hugging and kissing the kids and dancing with them. It looked like a great place to be. What a contrast!

'Do you think Mrs Jones would be a good teacher for Tom in reading?' asked the One Minute Manager.

'Of course,' said the entrepreneur.

'Why?'

'He didn't need a teacher in reading,' smiled the entrepreneur.

'That's right,' said the One Minute Manager. 'When you know what you're doing, you don't need a boss.'

'But if you have to have one,' laughed the entrepreneur, 'who wouldn't like a warm friendly one like Mrs Jones?'

'I said to Mrs McBride, "Tom isn't doing very well in maths. Could you straighten him out?"

' "Of course I could," she said.

' "How would you do it?" I inquired.

' "It would have been a lot easier," said Mrs McBride, "if I had had him from the beginning. I think he's discouraged now because it's harder than he thought it was and he's not doing well. So now when it's time for maths I would go over to Tom and say, 'It's maths time, Tom. Let's go over and get your maths folder.' (I don't think he even gets his own folder. I think he gets the folders of his friends who are absent just to mess them up.) Then I'd take him back to his desk and say, 'Tom, I want you to do problems one to three, and I'll be back in five to ten minutes to talk to you about your answers. If we work on this together, I know you're going to get better at maths.' "

'I said, "That's exactly what he needs! Would you please take over his maths?"

'And she did,' said the One Minute Manager.

'Did Tom do well with Mrs McBride's *coaching* style?' wondered the entrepreneur.

'He certainly did,' said the One Minute Manager. 'But do you think he enjoyed all that supervision and control?'

'No,' said the entrepreneur.

'That's the one thing I hate to report to the humanists of the world,' said the One Minute Manager. 'People do not learn skills by love alone.'

'What you're saying,' said the entrepreneur, 'is that if a person isn't competent to perform a particular task, then someone has to direct, control, and supervise that person's behaviour and if that prson's commitment is low, you also have to provide support and encouragement.'

'Luckily, in Tom's case,' said the One Minute Manager, 'there were only three months left in the school year. What do you think Mrs McBride's weakness was?'

'She was able to change her style from *directing* to *coaching*, but she could never change her style from *coaching* to *supporting* and *delegating*,' said the entrepreneur. 'She was great at start-up work but once children began to learn their maths skills, she wouldn't let them take more responsibility for their own learning.'

'**Y**OUR example with Tom not only clearly illustrates that development level is task or goal specific,' continued the entrepreneur, 'but it also suggests that a particular leadership style, which is appropriate with a person at one moment in time, may be inappropriate with the same person later on.'

'Definitely,' said the One Minute Manager, 'particularly when it comes to the *directing* and *coaching* styles. Your goal as a manager should be to gradually increase the competence and confidence of your people so that you can begin to use less time-consuming styles – *supporting* and *delegating* – and still get high-quality results.'

'How does that change in leadership style occur?' wondered the entrepreneur.

'First let's look at a model of Situational Leadership that shows the relationship between development level and leadership style.'

SITUATIONAL LEADERSHIP II

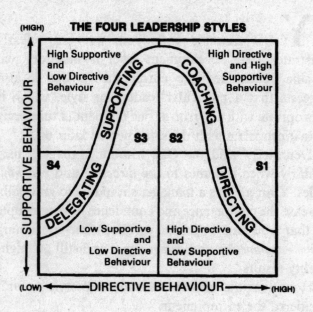

THE FOUR LEADERSHIP STYLES

(HIGH)

High Supportive and Low Directive Behaviour

SUPPORTING

COACHING

High Directive and High Supportive Behaviour

SUPPORTIVE BEHAVIOUR

S3   S2

S4   S1

DELEGATING

DIRECTING

Low Supportive and Low Directive Behaviour

High Directive and Low Supportive Behaviour

(LOW) ◄—— DIRECTIVE BEHAVIOUR ——► (HIGH)

HIGH	MODERATE		LOW
D4	D3	D2	D1

DEVELOPED ◄————————► DEVELOPING

DEVELOPMENT LEVEL OF FOLLOWER(S)

The entrepreneur studied the model closely. Then she looked up. 'Since you can draw a straight line up from D1 to S1, from D2 to S2, from D3 to S3, and from D4 to S4, the transfer from knowing the development level of a person on a particular task to the appropriate leadership style seems easy with this model.'

'Absolutely,' said the One Minute Manager. 'But let me make one other suggestion. In determining what style to use with what development level, just remember that *leaders need to do what the people they supervise can't do for themselves at the present moment.* Since a D1 has commitment but lacks competence, the leader needs to provide direction (S1-Directing); since a D2 lacks both competence and commitment, the leader needs to provide both direction and support (S2-Coaching); since a D3 has competence but variable commitment, the leader has to provide support (S3-Supporting); and since a D4 has both competence and commitment, the leader does not need to provide either direction or support (S4-Delegating).'

'That is a helpful suggestion,' said the entrepreneur. 'But what does the curve running through the four leadership styles mean?'

'We call it a performance curve,' said the One Minute Manager. 'As development level moves from D1 to D4, the curve shows how a manager's leadership style moves from S1 (directing) to S4 (delegating), with first an increase in support (S2), then a decrease in direction (S3), until eventually there's also a decrease in support (S4). At D4 the person is able to direct and support more and more of his or her own work. It's in this changing of leadership styles that the second secret of One Minute Management – One Minute Praisings – comes into play. Let me review the five steps you need to follow to develop a person's competence and commitment.'

'I'll bet the *first* step,' said the entrepreneur, 'is to *tell* them *what to do*.'

'Exactly,' said the One Minute Manager. 'The *second* step is to *show* them *what to do*, to model the behaviour. Once people know what to do, they need to know what good performance looks like. They need to know what the performance standards are.'

'Those two steps, telling and showing, are the key to One Minute Goal Setting, aren't they?' asked the entrepreneur.

'Yes,' said the One Minute Manager. 'Show and tell are also directive behaviours.'

'So training usually starts with some directive behaviours,' suggested the entrepreneur.

'Absolutely,' said the One Minute Manager. 'And once goals and directions are clear, the *third* step in developing people's competence and commitment is to *let them try*,' he added.

'But you don't want to turn over too much responsibility too soon, do you?' wondered the entrepreneur.

'No,' said the One Minute Manager. 'The risk has to be reasonable. That leads to the *fourth* step, observing performance. When you use a *directing* style you need to supervise closely and frequently monitor performance.'

'It seems to me that many managers forget this step,' said the entrepreneur.

'You're absolutely right,' said the One Minute Manager. 'Managers hire people, tell them what to do, and then leave them alone and assume good performance will follow. In other words, they abdicate; they don't delegate.'

'Unless the people you hire are both competent and committed,' said the entrepreneur, 'they will probably fail, or at least not perform up to the manager's expectations. When that occurs, most managers, out of frustration, would demand to know why things are not getting done or done well. Their questions seem unfair if people had assumed that being left alone meant the manager felt things were fine.'

'So you can see how skipping the "observe" step can be a disaster,' said the One Minute Manager. 'That's why we say around here that:

*

You Can
Expect More

If You
Inspect
More

*

'I'll bet the emphasis in your inspecting,' said the entrepreneur, 'is on catching people doing things right, not wrong.'

'That's why the *fifth* step in building competence and commitment is to *praise progress*,' said the One Minute Manager.

'So praisings are the key to helping people move from one development level to another, from D1 to D2, from D2 to D3,' said the entrepreneur, 'until gradually little external support from the boss is needed.'

'Let me show you a chart that illustrates exactly what you are saying – how a manager changes his or her behaviour as people's performance improves,' said the One Minute Manager, going to his desk. When he returned he handed the entrepreneur a sheet of paper.

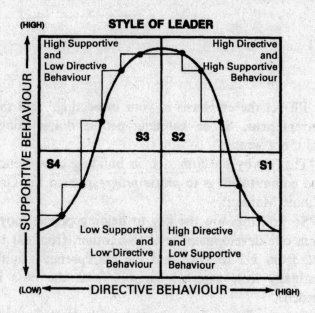

STYLE OF LEADER

(HIGH)

SUPPORTIVE BEHAVIOUR

High Supportive
and
Low Directive
Behaviour

High Directive
and
High Supportive
Behaviour

S3   **S2**

S4   **S1**

Low Supportive
and
Low Directive
Behaviour

High Directive
and
Low Supportive
Behaviour

(LOW) ◄── DIRECTIVE BEHAVIOUR ──► (HIGH)

HIGH	MODERATE		LOW
D4	**D3**	**D2**	**D1**

DEVELOPED ◄──────────► DEVELOPING

DEVELOPMENT LEVEL OF FOLLOWER(S)

'The steps moving up the curve show how the manager provides less and less direction as the subordinate learns his or her job,' said the One Minute Manager. 'Initially, more support is provided, but gradually the manager reduces the amount of support she or he provides as well, as shown by the steps going down the curve.'

'How can a manager cut back on supportive behaviour?' wondered the entrepreneur. 'Where do the people get their support?'

'From themselves or their colleagues,' said the One Minute Manager.

'When managers use a *delegating* leadership style,' wondered the entrepreneur, 'does that mean they are providing no direction or support for the person they are supervising?'

'The word "no" is too extreme,' said the One Minute Manager. 'Even in using a *delegating* style some direction and support are provided. But people who are competent and confident to perform at a high level (D4's) are generally not only able to direct their own behaviour but can catch themselves doing things right, too, because they've learned how to evaluate their own performance.'

'Is your strategy as a manager, then,' wondered the entrepreneur, 'to change your leadership style over time from *directing* to *coaching* to *supporting* to *delegating* as performance improves?'

'Yes,' said the One Minute Manager, 'as often as possible. But if progress is not made, I might have to back up and redirect the person until there's improvement. But my goal is to change my leadership style gradually, until my staff can perform their jobs well on their own with little supervision or support from me. Mao Tse-tung said it well:

*

'When The Best Leader's Work
Is Done,
The People Say,
"We Did It Ourselves!"'

*

'After talking with you and others in your organisation,' said the entrepreneur, 'that's a goal I will have for working with my staff. One question I have though is – What do you do in the beginning when you're first trying to develop someone and the performance is not even approximately right? Do you still praise that person?'

'No,' said the One Minute Manager.

'Do you ignore the poor performance?' asked the entrepreneur.

'No,' said the One Minute Manager. 'You go back to goal setting. You say, "I made a mistake. I must have given you something to do that you didn't understand. Let's backtrack and start again." '

'You mean you'd admit you were wrong,' asked the entrepreneur, 'and redirect the person?'

'Absolutely,' said the One Minute Manager. 'When you are training someone, besides praising, you have to be good at admitting you made a mistake.'

'So you're saying that if you care enough,' said the entrepreneur, 'you will admit that you were wrong and redirect the person. But what if you have to keep directing the person you are training time after time with little improvement in performance?'

'After a while,' said the One Minute Manager, 'you talk to the person about career planning and re-deployment.'

'That's interesting,' smiled the entrepreneur. 'So there are some people who cannot be trained for certain jobs?'

'Absolutely,' said the One Minute Manager.

'Well, I think I can see now where One Minute Goal Setting and Praisings fit into becoming a Situational Leader,' said the entrepreneur. 'Since development level is not a global concept, but task-specific, One Minute Goal Setting and the analysis of development level go hand in hand. At the same time, understanding a person's development level can help managers develop more reasonable performance standards. Praisings, on the other hand, are the key to developing people. By praising, you can gradually change your leadership from the directive styles of *directing* and *coaching* to the nondirective *supporting* and *delegating* styles. But where do Reprimands fit in?'

'**R**EMEMBER, you save Reprimands for D4's and D3's and occasionally D2's,' said the One Minute Manager, 'for people who were competent and committed but whose performance lately has not been up to par. Reprimands are not a training tool but a way to deal with motivation and attitude problems. If you use Reprimands with D1's, they will often lose their motivation and stop trying. Instead, use Reprimands with competent subordinates who have lost interest in a task.'

'So you're saying that Reprimands do not teach skills,' said the entrepreneur, 'but are only effective in getting good performers back in line when they develop a poor attitude towards their work.'

'That's right,' said the One Minute Manager. 'But remember, before you reprimand someone, make sure you have the facts and see that there are no extenuating circumstances. Sometimes a decline in performance is caused by a drop in confidence – the job is more complicated than anticipated. When that happens, you don't reprimand; you provide support and encouragement, and if necessary, direction.'

'It sounds as if you would recommend moving from a *delegating* style with a good performer,' said the entrepreneur, 'to a *supporting* style where you listen and gather data. And then, if you still don't get results, to a *coaching* style where you provide closer supervision and shorter time-lines, before moving to a *directing* style. Do you always recommend moving backward through the styles one at a time?' she asked.

'Most of the time,' said the One Minute Manager. 'Because if, in talking to the person, you gather any new information that explains the poor performance, you can always return to a *delegating* style without losing anything in terms of your relationship with the person. But if you go straight from a *delegating* style to a *directing* style, you are back into the old "leave alone-zap" leadership style. And if there is some reason for the poor performance, you are standing there with your foot in your mouth.'

'Let me see if I can summarise all this,' said the entrepreneur. She showed the One Minute Manager three reminder cards she had written up from her notes.

> **GOALS** start performance in the right direction and permit a manager to analyse a person's competence and commitment (development level) to perform well.

> **PRAISINGS** foster improvements in the development level of individuals and permit a manager to change his/her leadership style gradually from more direction (directing) to less direction and more support (coaching and supporting) to less direction and less support (delegating).

> **REPRIMANDS** stop poor performance and may mean that a manager has to move back gradually from less direction and less support (delegating) to more support (supporting) or more direction (coaching and directing).

**THE THREE SECRETS
OF ONE MINUTE MANAGEMENT
MAKE SITUATIONAL LEADERSHIP A
DYNAMIC MODEL**

'THAT'S a good summary,' said the One Minute Manager.

'OK. I've learned about flexibility and diagnosis,' said the entrepreneur. 'What about the third skill of being a Situational Leader, contracting?'

'Contracting is very important in making the whole system work,' said the One Minute Manager. 'One of the concerns that we've had with people who are learning how to be Situational Leaders is that they start using the concepts without telling anybody. For example, suppose I analysed your development level on a particular task as D4 – you were competent and committed. I really don't have to spend much time with you. I might stop coming to see you. After a while, what would you think?'

'I'd think that something was wrong,' said the entrepreneur, 'that you didn't care about me any more. I would feel ignored and unappreciated.'

'Precisely,' said the One Minute Manager. 'The same would be true with people at the other extreme – people who were very inexperienced. Suppose I decided they needed a lot more direction from me and I was in there telling them what, when, and how to do things all the time. If I continued to do that, what would they think after a while?'

'They would probably think you were picking on them,' said the entrepreneur, 'that you didn't trust them.'

'Then if one of them ran into you in the hall,' said the One Minute Manager, 'and you said that you hadn't seen me in a month, the other person would say, "No wonder – he's in my office all the time." So what would have been a good diagnosis and an appropriate leadership style is misinterpreted because I haven't told either individual why I am behaving the way I am. As an experienced, talented person, you'd think you'd done something wrong and the inexperienced person would probably think I didn't trust him. Suppose I had sat down with you and together we had decided that you really didn't need much supervision from me, that a *delegating* leadership style would be appropriate. Then, when I didn't come to see you, what would you think?'

'I'd think that it was fine because I'd know why you weren't coming to see me. The fact that you weren't supervising me much would really be a compliment to my skills and competencies,' said the entrepreneur.

'Right,' said the One Minute Manager. 'What do you think the inexperienced person would feel when I went to see him?'

'He would feel fine, too, because he would know that you were directing and closely supervising him now so that he could develop his skills. Eventually you'd be able to leave him alone,' said the entrepreneur.

'The importance of everyone's knowing what's going on is summarised in a phrase we share around here,' said the One Minute Manager.

*

*Situational Leadership
Is Not
Something You Do To People
But
Something You Do With People*

*

'I feel a sense of relief when I read that statement,' said the entrepreneur.

'I also used to think that as a manager I had to figure everything out by myself,' said the One Minute Manager. 'Contracting eliminated all that worry.'

'Where can I learn more about Contracting for Leadership Style?' asked the entrepreneur.

'Why don't you go see Alex Randall, our director of personnel,' said the One Minute Manager. 'He has organised our company's performance review system and I think he is best qualified to talk with you about contracting.'

'That sounds good,' said the entrepreneur. 'I'm anxious to learn more about contracting.'

WHEN the entrepreneur got to Alex Randall's office she found a distinguished-looking man who smiled and said, 'How can I help you?'

'The One Minute Manager told me you were the best person to teach me about contracting,' said the entrepreneur.

'I'd be happy to,' said Randall. 'Let me see if I can explain it this way,' he continued. 'There are three parts to performance review:

1. Performance Planning

2. Day-to-Day Coaching and Counselling, and

3. Performance Evaluation

'Contracting is part of performance planning and sets up day-to-day coaching and counselling, and yet which of those three steps do most companies start with in developing a performance review system?' asked Randall.

'Performance evaluation,' the entrepreneur said. 'Most companies ask the personnel department to develop a form for evaluation.'

'Then, once these companies have their evaluation form in place,' said Randall, 'they usually move to performance planning; that is, they hire or appoint someone from within to help people write goals. They fill notebooks with goals that nobody ever looks at.'

'How right you are,' said the entrepreneur. 'But One Minute Goal Setting has helped. All the unnecessary paperwork is eliminated when people set only three to five goals.'

'And which of the three parts of performance review almost never gets done in most organisations?' asked Randall.

'Day-to-day coaching and counselling,' said the entrepreneur.

'Right,' said Randall, 'but it's probably the most important step. Yet most managers and organisations forget to do it. The importance of day-to-day coaching and counselling comes to mind when I think of my favourite college teacher. He was always getting into trouble with the professor and other departmental members because on the first day of class he would hand out the final examination. The rest of the department would say, "What are you doing?" He'd say, "I'm confused." They would say, "You act it." He'd say, "I thought we were supposed to teach these people." They'd say, "You are, but don't give them the questions for the final exam." He'd say, "Not only am I going to give them the questions for the exam, but what do you think I'm going to do all term?" '

'Teach them the answers,' laughed the entrepreneur.

'Absolutely,' said Alex Randall, 'so when it came to the final exam, the students got top marks because they knew the answers.'

'It sounds as if your teacher wanted the students to win,' said the entrepreneur.

'That's what day-to-day coaching and counselling is all about,' said Randall, 'being responsive to the people you supervise. Once your staff are clear about their goals (they have the final exam questions), it's your job to do everything you can to help them accomplish those goals (learn the answers) so that when it comes to performance evaluation (the final examination), they get high marks.'

'That's a beautiful example of creating a "win-win" situation for your people,' said the entrepreneur. 'But how does that relate to contracting for leadership style?'

'As I said, the contracting process sets up day-to-day coaching and counselling,' said Randall.

'How does it work?' asked the entrepreneur.

'As usual, it all starts with goal setting,' said Randall. 'Suppose you were my wage and salary administrator. The process would start with us as individuals identifying three to five key goals for your operation. Then we'd develop performance standards for the next three to six months in relation to each goal.'

'Once you and I had identified goals separately,' said the entrepreneur, 'would we have a meeting to reach agreement on my goals?'

'Yes,' said Randall. 'Of course, you'd be more involved in goal setting on tasks where you were experienced and knowledgeable, a D3 or D4. On those tasks where you were a D1 or D2, I'd take the lead.'

'I imagine we'd agree not only on my areas of accountability but also on the performance standards for each area,' said the young woman.

'You're right,' said Randall. 'We'd agree on what a good job looks like. We'd also rewrite each goal so it was *SMART*.'

'What do you mean by SMART?' asked the entrepreneur.

'The *S* stands for *specific*. Goals should state exactly what the person is responsible for. The *M* stands for *measurable*,' said Randall.

'That's like the second part of One Minute Goal Setting,' added the entrepreneur. 'Subordinates need to know not only what they're being held accountable for but also how performance is going to be measured and what a good job looks like.'

'You're right,' said Randall. 'The *A* in SMART stands for *attainable*. The goals have to be reasonable. Whether or not they're reasonable depends on what's happened in the past.'

'Too many companies set goals that are impossible. I know I'm struggling with that in my own company. I know what I would like to achieve, but it's probably not realistic in the first few years,' said the entrepreneur. 'I suppose it's the same for individuals – you want to stretch them, but you don't want to make the goals so difficult that they're unattainable and the individual gets demotivated.'

'That's right,' said Randall. 'The *R* stands for *relevant*. As you remember, 80 percent of the performance you want from people comes from 20 percent of their activities. Therefore, a goal is relevant if it addresses an activity that makes a difference in overall performance. Finally, the *T* in SMART stands for *trackable*.'

'Trackable?' questioned the entrepreneur.

'As a manager you want to be able to praise progress,' said Randall. 'In order to do that you've got to be able to measure or count performance frequently, which means you need to put a record-keeping system in place to track performance.'

'SMART – that's really helpful,' said the entrepreneur. 'But what if there was disagreement about one of the goals and after some dialogue the disagreement didn't seem to be resolvable? Who decides?'

'The Golden Rule,' said Randall.

'The Golden Rule?' echoed the entrepreneur.

'Whoever owns the gold makes the rules,' laughed Randall. 'The boss decides.'

'Many managers stop the process after goal setting, don't they?' said the entrepreneur.

'Yes,' said Randall, 'and then managing by objectives becomes a licence to use the "leave alone-zap" leadership style.'

'I assume then that after setting goals and agreeing on measures and performance standards,' said the entrepreneur, 'we would contract for leadership style.'

'Yes,' said Randall. 'Since all my people know about Situational Leadership, the next step in contracting is for you and me individually to analyse your development level for each of the goals we agreed on and then to determine the leadership style you will need from me to succeed – that is, to perform at the desired level.'

'When you say "individually",' wondered the entrepreneur, 'does that mean I analyse my own development level?'

'That's right,' said Randall. 'And I will be doing the same thing. Then when we meet again our task will be to agree upon your competence and commitment with respect to each goal and to agree upon the leadership style you need. For example, suppose the three main goal areas for you were policy development, administration, and implementation. We'd set performance standards in each area, one at a time.'

'Then would you tell me what you think my development level is in relation to a standard in policy development, for example, and would I tell you what I think it is?' asked the entrepreneur.

'The rule is we'd agree on who goes first,' said Randall. 'If you go first, my job is to listen to your analysis and then before I can say anything, I have to tell you what I heard you saying.'

'That frees us to listen to each other,' said the entrepreneur.

'You've got it,' said Randall. 'Because if one of us is more verbal than the other, that person will dominate the conversation.'

'After both of us have been heard,' said the entrepreneur, 'I suppose we'd discuss similarities and differences in our analyses. If we cannot resolve our differences, does the Golden Rule still apply?'

'Not here,' said Randall. 'With development-level analysis, the nod goes to the subordinate. For example, if you feel you can be left alone, a D3 or D4, and I think you should be supervised, a D2 or D1, we would go along with your judgment – with one proviso. We'd have to agree on what the results will be for the next month so that we can both observe your performance.'

'In that case, I would probably work furiously over the next thirty days to prove that I was right,' said the entrepreneur.

'Which is exactly what I want to happen,' said Randall. 'I want you to be right.'

'After we have agreed on development level,' asked the entrepeneur, 'do we then agree on how you will supervise me?'

'Yes,' said Randall. 'Once development level is clear, leadership style falls into line. At the same time, you have to remember that the leadership style you decide on may be only temporary as you help your subordinates gradually stand on their own two feet and learn to direct and motivate themselves. Take a look at this Game Plan for Contracting for Leadership Style.

CONTRACTING FOR LEADERSHIP STYLE GAME PLAN

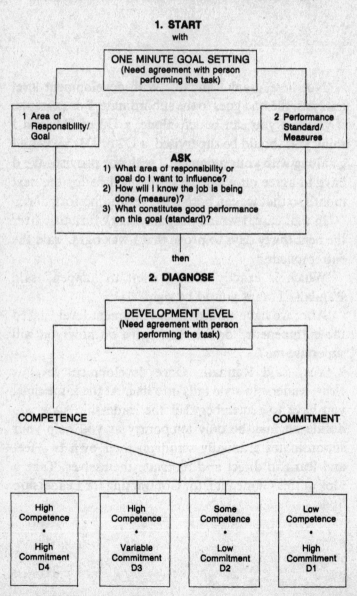

1. START
with

ONE MINUTE GOAL SETTING
(Need agreement with person
performing the task)

1 Area of
Responsibility/
Goal

2 Performance
Standard/
Measures

ASK
1) What area of responsibility or
goal do I want to influence?
2) How will I know the job is being
done (measure)?
3) What constitutes good performance
on this goal (standard)?

then

2. DIAGNOSE

DEVELOPMENT LEVEL
(Need agreement with person
performing the task)

COMPETENCE

COMMITMENT

High
Competence
•
High
Commitment
D4

High
Competence
•
Variable
Commitment
D3

Some
Competence
•
Low
Commitment
D2

Low
Competence
•
High
Commitment
D1

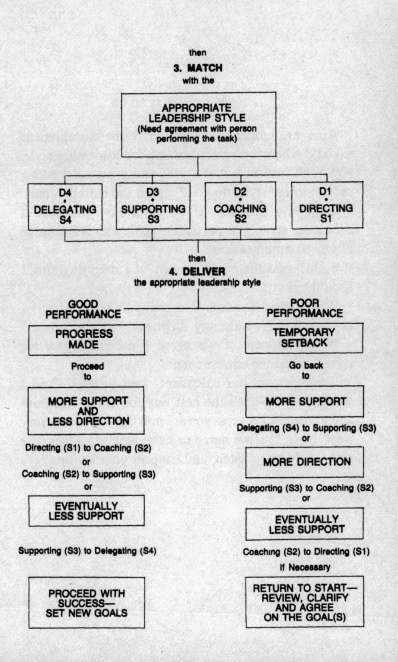

then

3. MATCH

with the

APPROPRIATE
LEADERSHIP STYLE
(Need agreement with person
performing the task)

| D4 • DELEGATING S4 | D3 • SUPPORTING S3 | D2 • COACHING S2 | D1 • DIRECTING S1 |

then

4. DELIVER
the appropriate leadership style

GOOD
PERFORMANCE

PROGRESS
MADE

Proceed
to

MORE SUPPORT
AND
LESS DIRECTION

Directing (S1) to Coaching (S2)
or
Coaching (S2) to Supporting (S3)
or

EVENTUALLY
LESS SUPPORT

Supporting (S3) to Delegating (S4)

PROCEED WITH
SUCCESS—
SET NEW GOALS

POOR
PERFORMANCE

TEMPORARY
SETBACK

Go back
to

MORE SUPPORT

Delegating (S4) to Supporting (S3)
or

MORE DIRECTION

Supporting (S3) to Coaching (S2)
or

EVENTUALLY
LESS SUPPORT

Coaching (S2) to Directing (S1)

If Necessary

RETURN TO START—
REVIEW, CLARIFY
AND AGREE
ON THE GOAL(S)

After examining the Game Plan, the entrepreneur
asked, 'When you're contracting for leadership style,
you don't just leave it at saying you'll use a *delegating*
or a *coaching* style, do you?' asked the entrepreneur.

'No,' said Randall. 'If we agree that you need a
delegating style on a particular goal, who is in charge
of our communication?'

'I am,' said the entrepreneur. 'If I need anything I
should tell you.'

'Right,' said Randall. 'The only rule is tell me early,
not late. I don't want any surprises.'

'What happens if we agree I need a *supporting*
style?' asked the entrepreneur.

'We'd get out our calendars,' said Randall, 'and I
would ask, "What's the best way for me to recognise
and praise the progress you are making – at lunch every
week or so?" If we agree to have lunch together, my
role would be to listen, and support your actions.'

'What if we had agreed upon a *coaching* style?' asked the entrepreneur.

'I would be in charge now,' said Randall. 'I might say, "Let's schedule two meetings a week for at least two hours to work on the goal you need help with – how about Monday and Wednesday from one to three P.M.?" With a *directing* style we'd be meeting even more frequently.'

'So the leadership style, once it's determined, establishes the number, frequency, and kind of meetings you have with your staff?' wondered the entrepreneur.

'Yes,' said Randall. 'What's nice about this system is that I might meet you for a couple of hours twice a week for a month and find you are catching on and starting to perform well on that goal. What leadership style should I now move to?'

'A *supporting* style,' replied the entrepreneur.

'Right,' said Randall. 'Then I'd ask you how you want your One Minute Praisings delivered.'

'Then if I continue to progress,' asked the entrepreneur, 'will you eventually move to a *delegating* style?'

'Precisely,' said Randall. 'I will keep changing my leadership style as long as you continue to grow and develop so at the end of the year we have not only a record of your performance but also a sense of your growth as evidenced by changes in my leadership style.'

'I can see why you say contracting for leadership style is the key ingredient to being an effective manager,' said the entrepreneur. 'Are there any other things I should know?'

'I think you know enough,' smiled Randall. 'Now you just need the courage to follow through on your good intentions.'

'That's easier said than done,' said the entrepreneur.

'I'd suggest you make one last visit to the One Minute Manager. He'll know how to build up your commitment,' said Alex Randall, smiling.

'That's a good idea,' said the entrepreneur, 'and thanks for your help.'

As the entrepreneur was walking back to see the One Minute Manager, she was struck by the simplicity and the power of what she had learned from Randall. She stopped several times to jot down thoughts that were going through her head.

When the entrepreneur got to the One Minute Manager's office, he greeted her with a smile. 'How did your discussion with Alex Randall go?'

'Very well,' said the entrepreneur. 'I'm fascinated by how much sense contracting for leadership style makes even though it's different from what I was taught in the management courses I've taken over the years.'

'Different in what way?' wondered the One Minute Manager.

'**Y**OU make a clear distinction between a leader's attitude and feelings about people and his or her behaviour towards them,' said the entrepreneur. 'We were always taught that when managers use a directive leadership style, they probably think their subordinates are lazy, unreliable, and irresponsible, and therefore need close supervision. But if managers use a participative leadership style, they believe their people are responsible and self-motivated. What I've learned from you is that positive assumptions about people are as given; you believe people have the potential to become high performers. What fluctuates is the manager's behaviour, depending on subordinates' needs for direction and support.'

'The key word is potential,' said the One Minute Manager.

'That's the beauty of it all,' said the entrepreneur. 'Now when I use a directive leadership style, I'll know it's not because I think that the person isn't any good. On the contrary, I'll think that the person has the potential to be a high performer – self-directed and self-motivated – but lacks experience. The person needs direction from me to begin developing his or her full potential.'

'That's an important lesson,' said the One Minute Manager. 'What you've learned is that positive assumptions about people can be expressed by using any of the four leadership styles, not just *supporting* or *delegating*.'

'I think it can all be summarised by this statement,' said the entrepreneur.

*

*Everyone
Is A
Potential
High Performer*

*Some People
Just Need
A Little Help
Along
The Way*

*

'YOU'VE got it,' said the One Minute Manager.

'And now I know it's up to me. Finally, I know how to develop my staff so I don't have to do all the work myself,' said the entrepreneur.

With that, the entrepreneur got up and shook the One Minute Manager's hand and said, 'Thanks for your help.'

'The only thanks I need,' said the One Minute Manager, 'is for you to do it – for you to use what you've learned – and to have it work for you. Remember the old Buddhist saying:

"To Know
And Not To Use
Is Not Yet To Know!" '

And use it she did. The entrepreneur went back to her company and told all the people who worked directly for her what she had learned and they in turn told the people who worked for them. Pretty soon the inevitable happened:

The entrepreneur became a Situational Leader.

She became a situational leader not because she thought like one or talked like one but because she behaved like one.

She started with clear goals.

Then with her staff, she diagnosed their competence and commitment to accomplish each goal without supervision.

Then she contracted with each of her members of staff on each of their tasks and together they decided which leadership style was appropriate.

Finally, she followed through and provided the leadership style they had agreed to until enough progress was made to warrant a change in leadership style.

Years later, the entrepreneur looked back upon the time she had spent learning to be a situational leader. It had made all the difference in her life at work and at home.

Her original company had now grown into eight separate enterprises. She was the Chair of a holding company and there was a managing director for each of her eight companies. While officially those managing directors reported to her, they really ran their own shows.

Two of them had had the competence and commitment from the beginning to direct their own operations. They kept the entrepreneur informed of the performance of their companies but she never interfered with their efforts unless they asked for her support or advice.

The other six managing directors were more or less competent and committed in the various aspects of running a company. The entrepreneur had worked closely with them through the contracting process and had varied her leadership style to fit the needs of the situation. She smiled now as she realised that she didn't have much to do any more because those managing directors could now run their own shows, too. She had helped them on the journey to becoming independent, self-motivated, high-performing managers.

The entrepreneur felt the same kind of success at home with her three children. Over time, they had all developed into independent, self-motivated people. Now that they were grown-up, the entrepreneur enjoyed being their friend more than their mother. That doesn't mean she wasn't there when they needed her, but now it was their initiative that motivated her involvement in their lives. She was happy that they still wanted to spend time with her.

The entrepreneur was happy and proud that she had learned the essence of good leadership from the One Minute Manager. She would never forget that effective managers have a range of management styles that they can use comfortably. They have developed some flexibility in using those styles in different situations. Effective managers also have a knack for being able to diagnose what their people need from them in order to build their skills and confidence in doing the tasks they are assigned.

Finally, effective leaders can communicate with their staff – they are able to reach agreements with them not only about their tasks but also about the amount of direction and support they will need to accomplish these tasks.

These three skills – *flexibility*, *diagnosis*, and *contracting* – are three of the most important skills managers can use to motivate better performance on the part of the people with whom they work. What the entrepreneur had built was an organisation in which people's contributions were valued. Her responsive style encouraged others to take risks and responsibility until, in time,

It was hard to distinguish who the entrepreneur was.

:01 *Praisings*

We would like to give a public praising to a number of important people in our lives:

Our associates and friends at Blanchard Training and Development, Inc. – *Margie Blanchard, Rene Carew, Calla Crafts, Fred Finch, Laurie Hawkins, Kelsey Tyson*, and especially *Don Carew* and *Eunice Parisi-Carew* for their support and synergistic thinking around the development of Situational Leadership II.

Pat Golbitz, Larry Hughes, and *Al Marchioni* at William Morrow, and *Margaret McBride*, our literary agent, for continuing to believe in the One Minute Manager concept.

Spencer Johnson, for his creativity and writing genius, which have inspired us.

Harvey Mackay for teaching us the true meaning of being an entrepreneur.

Eleanor Terndrup and *Vicki Dowden* for their dedication and typing skills, without which this book would never have become a reality.

Our mothers – *Dorothy Blanchard, Florence Kuiper*, and *Irma Zigarmi* – and our children – *Scott, Debbie*, and *Lisa* – for their unconditional love and support, which have made a tremendous difference in our lives.

About the Authors

Kenneth Blanchard: Few individuals have had as much impact on the day-to-day management of companies as has Kenneth Blanchard, co-author of *The One Minute Manager* and *Putting the One Minute Manager to Work*.

Blanchard, a popular speaker for national conventions, seminars, and business meetings, is a well-known writer, consultant, and teacher. His text *Management of Organizational Behaviour: Utilizing Human Resources*, now in its fourth edition, co-authored with Paul Hersey, is considered standard reading on the subject of management.

Dr Blanchard, with his wife, Margie, is the founder of a management consulting firm, Blanchard Training and Development, Inc., in San Diego. He also holds the position of professor of leadership and organisational behaviour at the University of Massachusetts at Amherst.

Blanchard earned his B.A. in government and philosophy from Cornell University, his M.A. in sociology and counselling from Colgate University and his Ph.D. in administration and management from Cornell.

Patricia Zigarmi is vice-president of Zigarmi Associates, Inc., and vice-president for consultant services/ product development at Blanchard Training and Development, Inc. Under her leadership, ongoing contracts were established with several major corporations including AT&T, Lockheed, Canadian Pacific Trucks, Chevron, Sprouse Reitz, and Beverly Hills Savings. Dr Zigarmi also coordinates seminar staffing and manages the product-development function for BTD.

Dr Zigarmi received her B.S. in sociology from Northwestern University and her doctorate in leadership and organisational behaviour from the University of Massachusetts at Amherst. In addition to her responsibilities at BTD, Pat has served as editor of the *Journal of Staff Development* and executive secretary of the National Staff Development Council, a professional association of staff-development coordinators in public schools across the United States.

Pat lives in San Diego with her husband, Drea, and daughter, Lisa.

Drea Zigarmi is the president of Zigarmi Associates, Inc., and the director of research and development for Blanchard Training and Development, Inc. His work has been critical to BTD's success with its clients. Almost every product that has been developed at BTD over the last four years has Drea Zigarmi's mark on it. Dr Zigarmi has co-authored with Ken Blanchard the well-known 'Leader Behaviour Analysis' instrument and the 'Development Task Analysis' form used in all Situational Leadership seminars.

Dr Zigarmi's clients include Canadian Pacific Trucks, AT&T, Lockheed, Chevron Oil Company, the Mellon-Stuart Company, and numerous fast-growing entrepreneurial companies. With these clients, Dr Zigarmi has managed long-term projects that have produced significant bottom-line results. The companies have successfully adopted management-development programmes, performance-appraisal programmes, and productivity-improvement projects built around the concepts of Situational Leadership.

Zigarmi received his B.A. in science from Norwich University and a master's in philosophy and doctorate in administration and organisational behaviour from the University of Massachusetts in Amherst.

Drea lives with his wife, Pat, and five-year-old daughter, Lisa, in San Diego.

Useful Addresses

Blanchard Training and Development, Inc. work worldwide with large and small companies to assist them in improving performance and increasing human satisfaction.

Services available include seminars ranging from two to five days; learning materials, from self-assessment instruments to audio and video programmes; and ongoing consultation, from team building to long-term productivity implementation.

For further information on these services please contact Blanchard Training and Development representatives:

Europe

Blanchard Training and
  Development UK
2 The Chapel
Royal Victoria Patriotic
  Building
Fitzhugh Grove
London SW18 3SX
Great Britain

Tel: 0181 871 2546
Fax: 0181 871 3866

Australia

The PTD Group,
Suite 403, 4th Floor
Henry Lawson Business
  Centre
Birken Head Point
Cary Street
Drummoyne
NSW 2047
Australia

Tel: (0061) 719 8955
Fax: (0061) 719 8930

The 22 Immutable Laws of Marketing

ALI RIES AND JACK TROUT

Al Ries and Jack Trout, two of the world's most successful marketing strategists, call upon over forty years of marketing expertise to identify the definitive rules that govern the world of marketing.

Combining a wide-ranging historical overview with a keen eye for the future, the authors bring to light 22 superlative tools and innovative techniques for the international marketplace. The authors examine marketing campaigns that have succeeded and others that have failed and why good ideas didn't live up to expectations, and offer their own ideas on what would have worked better. With irreverent but honest insights, and often flying in the face of conventional, but not always successful, wisdom, they give us:

The Law of Candour
be honest with your audience, point out the negatives, and improve your credibility

The Law of Line Extension
don't try to be all things to all people; companies that overextend themselves consistently lose market share

The Law of the Ladder
the battle isn't lost if you fail to be No. 1

The real-life examples, common-sense suggestions and killer instincts contained in *The 22 Immutable Laws of Marketing* are nothing less than rules by which companies will flourish or fail.

0 00 638345 9